THE STORY
——— OF ———
Christmas

Stephanie Jeffs
and John Haysom

A long time ago,

in a town called Nazareth,

something very special happened. . .

It had all happened so quickly.

Mary had been sweeping the floor when the angel came. It was something she did every morning, before the day grew too hot. Suddenly the room filled with the whitest of lights. It was unlike any other light she had ever seen, because, as she swung round, she was able to look straight into it.

'Mary,' the man had said. The sound of her name made her look up into the light. It was beautiful. She knew at once that this was an angel.

'Do not be afraid,' said the angel. 'God is with you. You have no reason to be afraid. I am Gabriel. I have come to tell you that God is pleased with you. You will become pregnant and have a baby boy—God's own Son. He will be the Saviour of the world.'

The words were incredible, but Mary did not doubt them.

And now, here she was, leaving the town of Nazareth with her fiancé, Joseph. She was expecting a baby she knew was not his, but God's.

A census had been ordered by the Roman Emperor, who wanted to know how many people lived in his land so he could tax them. They were going to Bethlehem with many other families because it was the town Joseph's family had come from: the city of David.

6

Joseph guided the donkey and helped
Mary as they travelled together.
When they finally saw the ancient town of
Bethlehem ahead of them, Mary felt relieved. But Joseph
could tell from a distance that the town was unusually
crowded. There were people everywhere. The whole town
was like a market place.

There was only one inn in Bethlehem. The noise from the
open windows indicated how full it was. So Joseph
was not surprised by the innkeeper's response.

'Have I got a room?' said the innkeeper. He looked hot and tired, and beads of sweat sparkled on his forehead. 'I haven't got a space anywhere. Try one of the houses.' He shut the door.

Joseph tried the houses. They were all full. It was hopeless. Before long he found himself back at the inn. He stopped outside the door and knocked again.

'Sir,' he said, before the innkeeper could speak. 'I know that you do not have any room in your inn, but my wife is pregnant and will soon give birth.

'I have tried everywhere, but, as you said, there is no room. Do you know of anywhere where we can rest tonight?'

The innkeeper wiped his forehead with the back of his hand. He looked at Mary and then at Joseph.

'I can only think of one place,' he said. He pointed to a building beside the inn. 'Stay there, if you want.'

'Thank you,' said Joseph. He turned round and pulled the donkey towards the stable.

It was dark in the stable (and smelly), but it was quiet and still away from the crowds. Mary tried to rest.

She felt her body tighten with pain and knew that very soon she would give birth to her special baby.

Joseph tethered the cattle at one end of the stable. He kicked away the dirty, soiled straw and scattered what was clean over the hard ground.

There, in the stable, Mary gave birth to her first child, a son. She took him in her arms and held him, while he took his first breaths of air. She smiled as he nuzzled against her, and she stroked the soft, dark hair on his head. She placed her little finger in the palm of his tiny hand and felt his gentle grip.

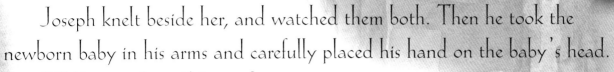

Joseph knelt beside her, and watched them both. Then he took the newborn baby in his arms and carefully placed his hand on the baby's head.

'Welcome, Jesus!' he said.

From where she lay, Mary ripped some cloth into long strips, which she wrapped around Jesus. Then she picked him up and gently laid him in the manger.

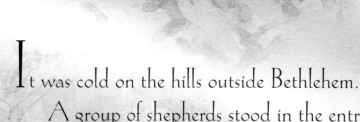

It was cold on the hills outside Bethlehem.

A group of shepherds stood in the entrance of the sheep fold.

The fire had almost died down, and all that remained were deep red, glowing embers.

Suddenly, a bright, dazzling light filled the night sky and a voice spoke from deep within the light, and echoed round the hillside.

'Do not be afraid!' said the voice. It was as if it were an order.

Instantly, a still peace came over the shepherds. They stopped trembling and slowly stood up. Within the light they saw the outline of an angel, which grew sharper and clearer as he spoke.

'I have good news for you and for the whole world!' said the angel. 'A baby has been born tonight in Bethlehem. He is God's Son, and he will save the world. You can go and see him for yourselves. You will find him wrapped in strips of cloth, lying in a manger.'

The angel had hardly finished speaking when the shepherds looked up and saw hundreds of angels. They danced across the sky, and as they danced, they sang.

'Glory to God in the highest heaven. Peace to his people on earth!'

The sound of the singing made the earth tremble, and the shepherds moved with the music of the song. They sang with the angels. 'Glory to God!' they sang, 'Peace on earth!'

Gradually the singing grew quieter, and the light became more dim, until the darkness of the night returned, and the shepherds found themselves standing alone on the hillside.

They remained rooted to the spot, until one of them finally spoke.

'Did the angel really say that God's Son has been born tonight?' he said, voicing the thoughts of them all. He looked around.

'Yes,' said another.

They stood in silence once more.

'Let's go!' said one of the shepherds, picking up his staff. He turned to his friends and he began to laugh. 'What are we waiting for? Let's go to find this baby in Bethlehem!'

The shepherds ran down to Bethlehem, and through the now empty, silent streets, until they found the stable.

They paused in the entrance and saw Mary and Joseph. Then they went in. There was no need to say anything. It was as if Mary and Joseph were already expecting them.

They gathered round the manger and saw the tiny newborn baby, swaddled tightly in strips of cloth, lying on the hay. Instinctively they sank to their knees.

'Glory to God!' they whispered.
'This is the Saviour of the world!'
'His name is Jesus,' Joseph told
them.

As the baby Jesus slept, the shepherds told Mary and Joseph everything that had happened that night. They talked about the angels and the song that they had sung. They talked about the birth of Jesus, God's own Son, and they praised God together for all that had happened.

As dawn broke, and the shepherds left the stable, Mary closed her eyes.
'Nothing is impossible with God!' she thought, and she lay back,
waiting to hear the morning cries of her newborn baby, Jesus.

Many miles away, in another country, some wise men were studying the stars. They searched through ancient charts and documents, until they were certain that what they had seen in the sky was true. A bright new star shone in the night sky. It had appeared suddenly and without warning. It was bigger and brighter than any other star in the universe.

'It is the star for a new king,' said one wise man to his friends, and he pointed to his chart. 'There is no doubt. This star shows that an important new king has just been born!'

The wise men looked at each other excitedly.

As quickly as they could, they packed provisions for their journey. They did not know how long it would take them, or where they were going.

But they were sure that if they followed the star, they would eventually find a new king. And because they were certain of what they would find, they brought with them presents of gold, frankincense and myrrh.

Eight days after the baby was born,
Mary and Joseph took him to be
circumcised.

'What will you call the child?'
Joseph was asked.

'His name is Jesus,' he replied.

Six weeks later, they loaded their
donkey to travel to the temple in
Jerusalem. It was not far away, and
although they had talked about returning
to Nazareth, they had decided to make
Bethlehem their home.

Joseph carried the two young doves
which he would give the priest to offer as a
sacrifice to God. An old man stared
intently at Mary and the baby she was

20

holding. He slowly made his way towards her, picking his way through the crowd. Mary handed Jesus to the old man. The man, whose name was Simeon, cradled the child in his arms, and then he spoke, his eyes overflowing with tears. 'Sovereign Lord,' he said. 'You have kept your promise to me. I have seen the Saviour of the world!'

He handed Jesus back to Mary. Mary and Joseph looked at each other. They were too amazed to speak.

At that moment, an old woman called Anna came up to them. She smiled and her face lit up with joy as she praised God.

Mary and Joseph made their way back to Bethlehem, thinking of all the things they had heard and seen in Jerusalem. They were unaware of the three other travellers who had begun their journey to visit them.

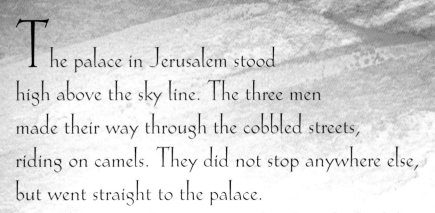

The palace in Jerusalem stood
high above the sky line. The three men
made their way through the cobbled streets,
riding on camels. They did not stop anywhere else,
but went straight to the palace.

King Herod was surprised to hear he had foreign visitors.
He was not expecting them. He was even more surprised when he
heard what they had to say.

'Sire,' they said, as they bowed before him. 'We have come to see the
new king, who has been born the King of the Jews. We saw his star rise in
the east, and we have come to worship him.'

Herod smiled. 'How interesting,' he said.
He left the three men and called his advisers.

'Tell me, does it say anything in our ancient
writings about where God's Saviour King will be
born?' asked Herod.

'In Bethlehem,' they replied.

'I am the only king!' thought Herod.

'This other king must be destroyed!'

He smiled as he returned to the three men.

'Our ancient Scriptures say the king you are looking for will be found in Bethlehem. Go there, and look for the child. But when you have found him, come and tell me where he lives, as I, too, would like to worship him.'

The three men left the palace and made their way to Bethlehem. They left Herod with thoughts of murder in his mind.

'Look!' said one of the men, as they stepped outside the palace, into the night. 'The star!'

There in the sky was the star which they had seen months before.

It hung in the sky like an arrow, pointing the way to Bethlehem, to where Mary and Joseph lived.

As soon as the three men saw the house, they knew they were at the right place. They knocked on the door, and Mary opened it.

She was not expecting visitors, and had never seen men like them before. But she was not surprised that they had come.

'You have come to see the child?' she asked.

They nodded, and she
ushered them in. Mary took
the child into her arms.

He stood firm and watched the
visitors.
    One by one they knelt before him,
and the little boy smiled.
    Then they unwrapped the
presents they had brought with
them.
        The little child clapped

The gold sparkled even in the dull light, and the smell of the myrrh and the frankincense filled the house.

Then they left, overjoyed that they had seen the baby king.

It was late, and the three men had yet to return to Jerusalem to see King Herod as they had promised. They stopped for the night and fell asleep thinking of everything they had seen in the tiny house.

When they woke the following morning, they were all uneasy.

'I had a strange dream,' said one, as they prepared to leave.
'So did I!' said another. 'I do not think we should return to Jerusalem.'
'Neither do I,' agreed the third. 'Let's go home another way.'

That night, Joseph, too, lay thinking about the three men.

He fell into a restless sleep. Suddenly, he sat upright.

It was still dark.

Gently, he woke Mary.

'Mary,' he whispered. 'Get up!'

Mary rubbed her eyes.

'I've had a dream,' said Joseph urgently. 'An angel came to me with a message. King Herod wants to kill Jesus. We must run away, to Egypt!'

As Mary got ready to leave, she felt frightened. She heard a voice speaking to her: 'Do not be afraid!' She thought of the times she had heard that voice before, and knew that God was with her.

Quickly, Mary and Joseph gathered up as many things as they could and loaded them on to their donkey. The gifts from the three men would provide more money than they could ever earn.

God would keep them safe. Then, putting Jesus on the donkey in front of Mary, they escaped together to Egypt.